# ninita's BIG WORLD

## The True Story of a Deaf Pygmy Marmoset

by SARAH GLENN MARSH

illustrations by STEPHANIE FIZER COLEMAN

Clarion Books

HOUGHTON MIFFLIN HARCOURT

Boston    New York

Clarion Books
3 Park Avenue
New York, New York 10016

Clarion Books is an imprint of Houghton Mifflin Harcourt Publishing Company.

hmhco.com

The illustrations in this book were created digitally.
The text was set in Cafeteria Primary HMH.

Library of Congress Cataloging-in-Publication Data

Names: Marsh, Sarah Glenn, author. | Coleman, Stephanie Fizer, illustrator.
Title: Ninita's big world : the true story of a deaf pygmy marmoset / by Sarah Glenn Marsh ; illustrated by Stephanie Fizer Coleman.
Description: Boston : Clarion Books, Houghton Mifflin Harcourt, [2019] | Audience: Age 4-7. | Audience: K to Grade 3.
Identifiers: LCCN 2018033896| ISBN 9781328770011 (hardcover) | ISBN 9780358057628 (E-Book)
Subjects: LCSH: Pygmy marmoset--Biography--Juvenile literature. | Animals with disabilities--Biography--Juvenile literature.
Classification: LCC QL737.P925 M365 2019 | DDC 599.8/4--dc23
LC record available at https://lccn.loc.gov/2018033896

Manufactured in China
SCP 10 9 8 7 6 5 4 3 2 1
4500747129

In loving memory of Kiowa Josephine (Kali),
who left pawprints all over my heart —S.G.M.

For Seth, always —S.F.C.

This is Ninita, a pygmy marmoset.
Pygmy marmosets are the smallest monkeys in the world,
but that's not all that makes Ninita special.

When Ninita was born, she opened her eyes for the first time
and saw beautiful trees, ferns, and flowers.
She smelled sweet orange blossoms and the musk of her mother's fur.
She yawned and tasted warm air on her tongue.

But she couldn't hear the squawking parrots on the branches overhead.
She couldn't hear the hum of mosquitoes and dragonflies.
She couldn't even hear her parents' voices.
Ninita was born deaf. Her parents left her when she was just three weeks old.

Ninita was scared.
She didn't know how to find food for herself
or how to groom her fur.
She saw other marmosets scurrying
around the nature sanctuary,
but she couldn't understand
what they were trying to tell her.

And she didn't know how to ask for help.

Ninita felt so alone.

But then something wonderful happened.

Kind humans brought Ninita inside,
and she found herself in a cozy new nest of her very own.
She even got a cuddly toy that kept her warm.

Ninita didn't need to hear the voices of her human friends to know she was safe now. Love wasn't a sound. It was warm blankets and ropes to climb on.

Every day, someone groomed
her pretty fur with a toothbrush.
The bristles felt just like a mother's claws.

Ninita loved her toothbrush massages.

Ninita also loved to eat.
She saw the other marmosets happily nibbling on bugs and lizards,
but she liked smooth yogurt and lumpy rice pudding.

Fluffy whipped cream was her favorite!

When she wasn't gobbling down tasty sweets,
curious Ninita scurried and hopped through her new surroundings.

Every table was a mountain to be climbed. Every smell was an invitation to adventure.

Some days, Ninita was a treasure hunter, always spotting something
new and shiny with her sharp eyes.

She was a brave explorer,
getting lost in tall grasses and
peeking inside dark and spooky caves!

Sometimes, when she followed her nose to interesting new places,

Ninita wished she had a marmoset friend to share in her adventures.

But she couldn't hear the other marmosets inviting her to play.

As Ninita grew up, the world outside still looked huge,
bursting with new things to discover.

And one day, it was time to trade in her old nest for a bigger, better one.

But there was someone else in the new nest already—
another pygmy marmoset who was almost as little as she was!

Ninita wasn't sure what to think of Mr. Big at first.
He moved his mouth a lot, but she couldn't understand him.

Then Mr. Big sat beside Ninita in her favorite flower pot.
Without ever hearing his voice, Ninita understood what he was telling her.

He wanted to be her friend.

Soon Ninita realized that her new friend liked to do all the things she did:
eat, climb on things, and play.

And while Ninita couldn't hear his chatter or whisper secrets to him,
she could climb as high as he could and jump just as fast.

Ninita's world would always be silent, but that meant she noticed things the other marmosets often missed.

Like colorful creatures even smaller than she.

Ninita still liked to swing in and check on her human friends from time to time.

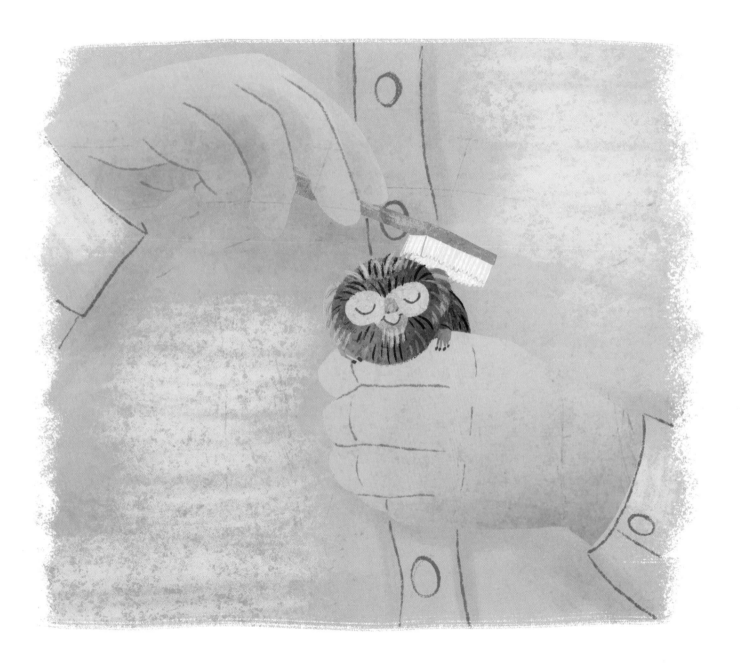

And she still loved her toothbrush more than anything else.

But she was happiest when she was outside, exploring with Mr. Big, the marmoset friend she'd always wanted!

Now love is a shared treat and napping
in the same hammock.

There's a big world surrounding Ninita's new nest,
and she's ready to climb, see, and taste it all.

As long as she can still curl up with her toothbrush at the end of the day.

# AUTHOR'S NOTE:

# More on Marmosets and the Rare Species Conservatory Foundation

Rare Species Conservatory Foundation

Ninita means "little girl" in Spanish, and it's fitting for such a tiny creature! As a baby, Ninita was smaller than a person's thumb. As a full-grown marmoset, she still fits easily in the palm of a person's hand and weighs only about as much as fifteen jelly beans. She lives at the Rare Species Conservatory Foundation (RSCF), a 501(c)(3) nonprofit organization located in Loxahatchee, Florida. Ninita and her parents are part of the

RSCF's effort to help the pygmy marmoset species. She was born in 2012 as part of their captive breeding program, which aims to conserve species that may not otherwise survive in the wild. This program also helps with education and research on select species, and RSCF is home to the largest captive population of pygmy marmosets in the United States.

Pygmy marmosets typically live in "family groups" composed of a mother, father, and several siblings. All adult members of the family group help care for baby marmosets until they are one year old, at which time they are no longer considered juveniles.

However, Ninita's parents left her when she was just three weeks old because they didn't understand why she wasn't doing the things they thought she should be; they didn't know that she was deaf, so they couldn't figure out how to care for her.

Once Ninita was safe in the hands of her human caregivers, they knew she would eventually need the company of another pygmy marmoset to be truly happy. They selected Mr. Big as her companion when both marmosets were just a few weeks old. The caregivers—playing monkey matchmaker!—introduced Ninita to Mr. Big when they were both a little older and ready to begin a family group of their own.

The native habitat of pygmy marmosets like Ninita is the Amazon rainforest. While they aren't yet endangered, they're currently listed as a species of special concern. They face habitat loss due to human industries. And because they're so cute and cuddly, they are often victims of the pet trade. Pygmy marmosets aren't domesticated and will not thrive as house pets, yet some people take advantage of their adorable looks by breeding and selling them. Although Ninita was raised by kind human caregivers, she was not and has never been a pet! Pygmy marmosets, even ones as special as Ninita, are happiest in their natural habitat.

While Ninita is the only known deaf pygmy marmoset in the world, it's possible there have been others like her born in the wild. Luckily for Ninita, being born in captivity gave her the chance to survive, as she was hand-reared by the zoologists at RSCF. Ninita reached maturity at two years of age and will hopefully continue entertaining her adoring fans with her antics and her toothbrush for years to come.

Visit the RSCF website at www.rarespecies.org to learn more about this wonderful organization and their campaigns to preserve global biodiversity. There you'll also find a wealth of educational resources, photographs, and ways that you can help save amazing animals like Ninita.

## SELECTED BIBLIOGRAPHY

Cawthon Lang, Kristina. *Primate Factsheets: Pygmy marmoset (Callithrix pygmaea) Taxonomy, Morphology & Ecology.* National Primate Research Center, University of Wisconsin-Madison, 2005.

Dunn, Mary R. *Pygmy Marmosets (Monkeys).* North Mankato, Minnesota: Capstone Press, 2013.

The Rare Species Conservatory Foundation of Loxahatchee, Florida. Read more at www.rarespecies.org.

The San Diego Zoo: Pygmy Marmosets. Read more at www.animals.sandiegozoo.org/animals/pygmy-marmoset.

Photo credit Dr. Paul Reillo

*The author and Ninita.*

# FUN FACTS ABOUT PYGMY MARMOSETS

### LIFE SPAN

They can live up to twelve years in the wild and eighteen years in zoos.

### WHERE TO FIND THEM

Pygmy marmosets are native to Brazil, Colombia, Peru, Ecuador, and Bolivia.

### HABITAT

Pygmy marmosets love rivers, rainforests, and bamboo thickets. They need plenty of hiding places because of their small size, but they never stray too far from the same few trees during their entire lives!

### DIET

Pygmy marmosets have super-sharp teeth for gouging holes in the trees they climb. They drink the tree sap for a delicious meal. During its lifetime, a marmoset might make hundreds of holes in the same tree.

They also like to eat butterflies, which sometimes land near their sap holes, as well as small lizards, worms, fruit, and veggies. At zoos, they also enjoy hard-boiled eggs!

### NATURAL CLIMBERS

Pygmy marmosets' tails are longer than their bodies. This helps them keep their balance as they swing and climb.

They also have sharp claws that help them hold on to tree bark.

### FAMILY MATTERS

Pygmy marmosets live in family groups composed of a mother, father, and several siblings.

When a new marmoset is born, the father carries the baby on his back for the first two weeks of its life. Older siblings help care for the younger ones to learn how to be good parents themselves someday.

### PREDATOR DANGER

Pygmy marmosets in the wild are hunted by cats, eagles, hawks, and some poisonous snakes that like to climb the same trees as the monkeys.

Luckily, the marmosets can turn their heads backward to check for danger. They can also leap really fast to get out of harm's way!

### MARMOSET CHATTER

Pygmy marmosets call to one another using clicks and chirps that mean everything from "Hello!" to "Danger!"

Sometimes their calls are too high-pitched for humans to hear.

### MARMOSETS AREN'T SO DIFFERENT FROM US

Pygmy marmosets make faces to express emotions, such as surprise, happiness, and fear. Just like humans, they move their lips and eyes to show how they're feeling.